MARJORIE C

CHILDREN ARE
LIKE OLIVE PLANTS

*What every parent
should know*

Unless otherwise indicated, all scripture quotations are taken from the King James Version of the Bible.

**Children Are Like Olive Plants
What Every Parent Should Know**

Copyright ©2002 by Marjorie O Esomowei

Publishing History

First Edition June 1994 (Fourth Man Publications)
Second Edition September 2002 (Wisdom Communications Ministries)

ISBN: 0-9543174-0-8

Printed in the United Kingdom 2002

A Publication of Wisdom Communications Ministries
P O Box 6071
Basildon
Essex SS14 1YQ

Acknowledgements

How can I ever say thanks? My Lord Jesus you have been so good. Thanks more than a million times. It can only take knowing you to be so courageous. Lord thanks again.

Thanks to the best gift the Lord gave me after my salvation, my husband, mentor and best friend - Rev. Clem Esomowei.

Many thanks for everyone who has taken time out to pray for my husband and I. Thank you for standing with us. Sincere thank you to Shade Phillips for your valuable contributions to the book.

Dedication

This book is dedicated with thanksgiving to Rhema and Maranatha Esomowei, our promised reward from the Lord.

Foreword

The importance of moral scriptural teachings in the lives of children of our time cannot be over emphasised. In recent years we can see children who grew up before our eyes becoming gang leaders, drug addicts, terrorists, sexual perverts and murderers. It would require a generation of parents and teachers with vision and concern for the future of our world to instil child discipline and moral scriptural instruction for the betterment of our world.

The removal of scriptural instructions from our school assembly lines in the past years has resulted in the upsurge of every evil vice of society. There must be a strong contention by the spirits of the underworld for the souls of our children which can only be countered by a combination of efforts by parents, teachers and ministers of God.

Children are like Olive Plants by Pastor Marjorie Esomowei who is my beloved cherished wife, best friend and co labourer in ministry is a vivid account of her ministry with children over a decade and half challenging parents and adults to a life of concern in prayers, instruction and mentorship. Children must be treated and cared for as God's heritage and not as another little "burden". Every President, Prime Minister, Monarch, Bishop, Pastor, Business executive, cabinet minister was once a child. That child you are looking after may be destined to be a world changer. Why not treat them as such now?

Pastor Clem Esomowei
Triumphant Church International

Introduction

We do not need to look far to realise that the devil is after the future generation and that the hearts of Christian parents are crying out for readable and easy information on how to greatly impact this next generation for our Lord Jesus Christ.

Apart from selling out on the original copies of **Like Olive Plants**, a revised copy of Like Olive Plants has become necessary as the need for such a book to provide valuable information for parents and carers of young children in these times cannot be over emphasised. Moreover the prompting of the Holy Spirit to review this book has been stronger than ever. I am sure you noticed that the name has also changed to **Children Are Like Olive Plants…. What every Parent should know.**

The voice of the Spirit comes to me in a song as I write to the body of Christ. (i.e. Parents, School Teachers, Sunday school teachers, Youth workers etc) "Christians wake no longer sleep. Shall we rest while others work? Shall we sit with folded arms when the Lord Himself commands". **Children Are Like Olive Plants** is a wake up call for us all to rise up and fortify the future of the upcoming generation and take back that which has been lost. Whilst we have sat down to criticise the younger generation and send them away from our Churches with our religious attitude, the world has gladly welcomed them and fed them with all kinds of ideologies that have slowly taken them away from Church.

As I do the review I have once again had to battle with the fact that not having children of my own, my book might be ridiculed for lack of experience. I only write because I have been commanded to write and as the Lord would often tell me, so do I also say to anyone who might have any reservations "Paul wrote so much about women, marriage and women in ministry taking a very strong stand on each of these issues yet he had no wife" If Apostle Paul blessed you by the inspiration of the Holy Spirit then I just might bless you too!

I currently spearhead a Prayer initiative with the intention of increasing the move of the Holy Spirit in the schools and higher Institutions of United

Kingdom. The most effective way for this move to take place will be for the bible to be read and taught publicly in the schools both by the teachers and the children themselves and for prayer to return back to our schools.

Beloved I pray that this type of prayer initiative would not be an isolated case but that after reading Like Olive Plants, it will be a wake up call for you! Now you know my heart please read and be blessed.

You might be wondering how I got into children ministry? In my late teen years, the Lord gave me an encounter, which I believe opened the way for me to minister to children. As a backslider, I had just completed my 'A' Levels examination and having missed admission into university, I had to work with the Nigerian Television Authority in Sokoto State as a programme producer.

On my resumption day, I was asked to present "The Children's Time", a weekly entertainment programme for children as the main producer was away sick that day. Just a few minutes to the airtime, we were told that the programme might not be aired if the sound mixer did not arrive. I really cannot say who started it, but suddenly we all were crying (i.e. the children and I), because of the likely postponement of the programme.

All other producers and the station crew were shocked at the fact that I as the producer of the programme was crying with the children. The sound mixer finally arrived, the programme was aired and it was very good. A strong bond was developed between the kids and I. They were glad to have someone who could identify with them all the way. My boss and other crewmembers instantly voted me to take over the programme, as they believed that the kids and I would get along very well. We did get on very well. Though a backslider at that time, I believe the Holy Spirit used those kids to open up something in me, which was my launching into the Children's Ministry.

A few years after this event, back to the church as a born again Christian, I again felt the burden to work with children and registered with my local church as a Children's Teacher. I remembered the fun of playing with the kids back at the television station and so concluded that the fun in the children's section was in the hand clapping, dancing, laughter and playing. There was a lot of energy burnt up every Sunday but still I relish the exciting times with Jesus in the midst of those kids.

I did not realise at this time that there was more to it than the hand clapping, dancing and all. But God has taken me step by step in the knowledge of His will concerning ministry to children. Several lessons have been learnt over the years like the word says in Isaiah 28:10

"For precept must be upon precept, precept upon precept, line upon line, line upon line, here a little, and there a little:"

TABLE OF CONTENTS

Acknowledgement
Dedication
Foreword
Introduction

CHAPTER 1

MY FIRST LESSON

> Joel 2:28
>
> ***And it shall come to pass afterward, that I will pour out my spirit upon all flesh; and your sons and your daughters shall prophesy, your old men shall dream dreams, your young men shall see visions:"***

In the children's department of my former church, I was given the responsibility to teach the children between ages 10 and 13 at that time as well as have oversight of the entire department administratively.

On a particular Sunday in 1986, I came to church expecting the same kind of fun like I was used to. I thank God that there was fun but not just the type I was used to. He did more and I give the Lord glory for this.

On this Sunday, service was rather long in the adult church and we had completed every activity planned for the day in my class. We needed to keep the children occupied for the remaining time so I asked the Holy Spirit "what's next?" He replied, "I have whispered several things to the children, which they will share if you ask them". . I was taken aback because this was a new area for me. I had never really known that God talked to children in this day and age. I did ask the children, not knowing what really to expect, but only in obedience to the sweet Holy Spirit

The first response came from a boy who asked us to pray for our country, Nigeria. I asked him to pray and his prayer was specifically on deliverance from the operations of armed bandits and night marauders. The next response also came from this boy. His message was again specific. God wanted a girl in the class to go home and make up with a neighbour whom she vowed never to forgive in spite of the fact that our lesson in the class all through that month was on forgiveness. Instantly a girl stood up crying with repentance because God had ministered to her heart. She reconciled with the woman on her street that day. It was a beautiful experience. It immediately dawned on me that this was another stage in my experience with God.

Shortly after the boy spoke, about six children in the class began to scream, "Sister Marjorie, there is fire all over my body, something is moving in my body." I had not bargained for this and for a moment I was confused. Just then the Holy Spirit led the Pastor of our Children's Church, into my class and when he saw the state of things, he said "Sister Marjorie, this is no longer children's church, please shut the door and let no one leave". He immediately raised up both hands and simply said "Jesus, defend your gospel".

Suddenly the class went wild. Several of those lovely children began to behave in ways that no one could have believed ordinarily. The works of the devil were exposed and many were set free by the power of the Holy Ghost and began to speak with other tongues. I learnt a big lesson that day. The message was clear; there was a battle for the hearts of our children. Even as God is interested in them, so also is the devil. The devil seeks to destroy them as prey but God has given them abundant life according to his riches in glory by Christ Jesus. That day I determined that no child will come in contact with me and remain the same. I decided to partner with God in the battle for the lives of our children.

This battle becomes more real in my heart as I see the things that happen in the world today. I pray that the Church will hear the call of the Spirit to stand in the gap for our children and the generation to come. Read the newspapers and listen to the news report and see some of the evil that is being perpetrated against children. Initially it appears like these children have no faces, but when such things begin to happen to faces that you can personally put a name to, then it is coming nearer home. Wake up women and men of God and fight for God's heritage.

Psalm 127:3
"Lo Children are an heritage of the Lord: and the fruit of the womb is His reward"

I am greatly encouraged that this battle is already won because of the work of Jesus Christ our Lord and Saviour at Calvary.

It might interest you to know that two of those children in my class are currently senior pastors of Churches and many others are active in various churches and ministries

Before I continue to the next chapter, I would like you to ask yourself "how much time do I spend praying for my children?" The Sunday school class at Church is only for two or so hours a week and cannot take the place of parental authority. Your children need your prayer cover everyday and no one else can stand in the gap for them like you would. This is not a cry of 'wolf wolf' for a wolf that does not exist but rather it is a Joel 2:15-17 call to parents to pray for their children and be alert to what God wants to do in our time.

CHAPTER 2

THE UNBORN CHILD IN
PREPARATION

The question of when a child becomes a real person has been an age long debate. This argument can only be authenticated from the holy Bible, which is the word and dictates of the Maker of all flesh, Creator of heaven and earth and of all living beings. The manufacturer's manual for a product is the most logical place to get accurate information about the design and purpose of the product. Our Lord Jesus categorically tells us in *John 10.10* that "I have come that they may have life". We are life givers and not life takers. The blood of children aborted will cry out to God from the ground just like the blood of Abel cried out to God except perpetrators repent.

Psalm 139:13 (NKJV) " For you formed my inward parts ". This bible verse confirms the integrity of the unborn child. The psalmist David speaks about the life of his embryo and the records of his body substance even before they were formed. What more do we need to know? *Psalm 139: 16 (*NKJV*)* " Your eyes saw my substance being yet unformed" <u>No one has permission to kill children whom God sees and records in His mind as human life</u>. The guilt of abortion is so strong that it can only take the redemptive blood of Jesus to wipe it off. ***Gen 9: 5*** " From the hand of every man's brother will I require the life of man" Does that not scare you? You may decide to use man's freewill as a free moral agent but the choice of abortion is a distortion of the use of your freewill. The simple truth is that those who propose abortion should be ashamed of themselves. Thank God that the blood of Jesus has cleansed us from our past sins. I was guilty of this sin but I thank God that the blood of Jesus has given me a clean slate.

Many times the doctors argue that abortions can be allowed in the case of abnormalities in Children during pregnancies. However we know that doctors can be wrong sometimes with their diagnosis. I quote an article by Carmen Wittmeir in Alberta report of May 17th 1999 (Now **THE REPORT** ... Canada's Independent News magazine) titled "The doctors are often wrong". "In 1998, the unborn daughter of Lana and Arrigo Monai of Edmonton was diagnosed in Utero with a rare genetic disorder and given a zero

– 5% chance of surviving. Despite lacking part of her fifth chromosome, Abigail defied the odds and entered the world breathing on her own. Although doctors feared she would suffer from heart diseases, spina bifida, digestive disorders and mental deficiencies, Abigail appears to be a normal, healthy, six-month-old today. "I feel sad for parents who choose abortion," Mrs Monai says. "They'll live with a significant loss for the rest of their lives."

The same article tells about "When Christine Friesen of Calgary looks at her energetic 10-month old son Joseph, she often thinks, "You almost weren't here." Mrs Friesen and her husband Mark, scheduled an abortion after being told their unborn child carried the mutilated X chromosome associated with Duchene muscular dystrophy, an incurable disease characterised by degenerating muscle tissue. "I couldn't allow my son to slowly suffer from the disease that killed my brother," Mrs Friesen says. However when the clinic was unable to abort her pregnancy on the scheduled day, the Friesens changed their mind. That minor inconvenience over a year ago has turned into a major blessing for the Friesens. To the surprise of experts across the country, Joseph was born completely healthy.

Even her doctor, Mrs Friesen says, wept in relief when the test results came back negative....Mrs Friesen warns that "anything can happen," especially since doctors are "only human." "It's sobering to think how close we came to not having Joseph," Mrs Friesen remarks. "There isn't a day that goes by in which we're not thankful for him"

Doctors can be wrong about their predictions on abnormalities. Again, testimonies abound of where many Christian women have stood on the word of God and come through unrighteous predictions during pregnancies. Abortion is not a way out because every child that is born into this world is a reflection of God's faithfulness to the people he has created. If God has given up on mankind he would not send more children into the world. Glory be to God in the highest.

The Scriptures confirm that we all existed even before we were formed in our mother's wombs. God said to Jeremiah,

> Jeremiah 1:5
> ***"Before I formed thee in the belly I knew***

thee; and before thou camest forth out of the womb I sanctified thee, and I ordained thee a prophet unto the nations."

If we know and believe this, then we have got no business at all participating in abortion. If we do so, we count ourselves guilty of eliminating people who are already existing in God's records and working as agents to thwart God's plan. Like Jeremiah, God knew us before we were formed in the womb.

Psalm 139: 13-15
*For you formed my inward parts;
You covered me in my mother's womb...
My frame was not hidden from you, when
I was made in secret*

A quick reminder about Jacob and Esau will go a long way to help us here. These two had their personalities even before their birth, which they held on to till they were older men.

May I go further to say that for those still expecting to have children of their own, faith should arise that these promised children are already in existence and are only waiting to be manifested in due season. It may interest you to know that the children unborn can be named and prayed for prophetically by name even before conception, so that they may turn out to be who God wants them to be,

Romans 4:17
"......... for faith calleth the things that be not as though they were"

Jeremiah 1:15
"Before I formed thee in the belly I knew thee; and before thou camest forth out of the womb I sanctified thee, and ordained thee a prophet unto the nations.

Luke 1:15
"For he shall be great in the sight on the Lord, and shall drink neither wine nor strong drink; he shall be filled with the Holy Spirit, even from his mother's womb."

In my mind, I believe a parent's attitude towards the child in the womb could make a whole lot of difference. The Bible says, "death and life are in the power of the tongue" (Proverbs 18:21).

Parents are mandated to pray for unborn children, asking for their sanctification unto good works and speaking God's promises upon their lives so that as John the Baptist and Jeremiah, our children will be separated unto good works even from the mother's womb. You do not have to wait until they are born before you begin to pray. Start now because children could be estranged from the womb. Psalm 58:3 ***"The wicked are estranged from the womb: they go astray as soon as they be born, speaking lies"***.

In my work as a children teacher, I have had cause to see obvious differences in children over whom their parents prophesied the promises of God daily before they were conceived and after conception. The difference when compared to other babies is so apparent. I implore all those trusting God for children to do the same as we prepare to bring our children into the world. Your testimony is on the way.

CHAPTER 3

CARETAKERS

> Psalms 127:3 – 4
> *"Lo, children are an heritage of the Lord: and the fruit of the womb is His reward. As arrows are in the hand of a mighty man, so are the children of the youth".*

To help me illustrate the caretaker role of parents I would use the practice of Nigerians with regards to soft drinks containers. Containers for soft drinks could be glass or plastic. At a quick glance they both look the same – they are just soft drink containers.

However in Nigeria, if you purchase soft drinks in glass bottles, you are obligated to return the bottles to the bottling company whilst plastic bottles are not returned. Therefore, the manner in which consumers treat the containers would highly depend on whether they would have to answer to the bottling company or not. For the plastic containers, since there is no return policy it is found littered all over the streets of Nigeria. People are more careful with the glass bottles because they know they shall give account to the bottling company someday.

In the same vein children are like these glass containers for whom someday we shall be answerable to their creator God. Caring for God's heritage requires commitment that will entail nourishing and adequate thoughtfulness towards your child. It is a love relationship resulting from the originator of love Himself. Children are God's heritage and His reward so they deserve every care that is due to that which is a heritage of God.

We need to treat our children as gifts sent from the Father to bless and brighten our homes. You know how you treat all your beautiful gifts. You need to do much more with God's heritage.

They are like arrows *(Psalms 127:4)* in the hands of a mighty man ready for use in battle. Arrows paint a picture of strength and security and we know that a dull and narrow arrow is of no use in battle. Caretakers should **lovingly** but firmly rear and train children to be loaded with the word of God ready to face the enemy at the gate.

We are not expected to raise timid and fearful children. We live in dangerous times and Christian Children should be affirmed more at home and Church and told who they are in Christ. I know a Christian couple that would always make their children say, "The righteous are as bold as a lion". Your children need to know that they worship a God who loves them enough to die for them and would have died for them even if they were the only one on earth. They should be as arrows, strong and ready to pierce the enemy.

Remember they are also like olive plants *(Psalm 128:3)* round about our table, tender and secure. What a contradiction from arrows – firm and strong in the hands of a mighty man and also tender plants that need to be nurtured, loved and provided for.

God in His infinite mercies is telling you that there has to be a balance in your responsibility of child upbringing. You need His wisdom to make every child of yours a rear combination of arrows and olive plants. This will make them kind and tender hearted enough to be humane in all their dealings and at the same time bold enough to face the challenges of this ever-changing world. They will exhibit the fruit of the spirit and also manifest as warriors in the Lord's army.

As a caretaker you need to specially ask for the enabling power of the Holy Spirit to achieve these results. We want our children to be as wise as serpents and at the same time, peaceful as doves – wonderful combination. One day we shall have to give account to God of how we cared for His heritage. Children, like adults are also spirit, soul and body and in taking care of them we should have this in mind to enable us to produce the total child.

Everything you do in your role as caretakers in teaching or training should be targeted towards the children's submission to the Lordship of Jesus Christ and to God Almighty, for the fear of God is the beginning of wisdom. **Psalm 144: 12** (NKJV) "That our sons may be as plants grown in their youth; that our daughters may be as pillars sculptured in palace style". God wants them to be balanced children who have a positive self esteem and self worth that is based on information from the scriptures.

> Matthew 19:14
>
> **"Suffer Little Children and forbid them not, to come unto me: for of such is the Kingdom of heaven.**

Nuggets for Parents and Carers?

1. Know that children belong to God and He is interested in their wellbeing.

2. Ask God for wisdom to raise children that will effectively affect their generation. Recently at a prayer meeting for schools, one of the speakers clearly stated that we need wisdom as parents to reconcile the children's knowledge from church to their secular experience. If this is not done we shall end up raising a generation of young Christians that are mute and have nothing to say to their world. Read Mark 9:14-29 (the child with the mute spirit). Through prayer and fasting you can empower your children communicate their faith to their peers and make their faith relevant to their world.

We need it in this age, where children are faced with greater pressures from their peers and the world they interact with everyday. We have to admit that most of the struggles that children face today were not there even ten years ago. That's why your children need your attention by way of bible studies, prayers, and discussions. They need you not just things, which you can give to them.

3. Make yourself available so that they can share their needs and worries with you and together you can solve the problems that make them cry themselves to sleep.

4. Avoid criticising your children; rather let both parents spend time praying for them. Jesus prayed for Peter so that the devil may not crush him. Take delight in praying for your children.

5. Be interested in children in your community. Apart from praying for your children you should also pray for your neighbour's children too.

CHAPTER 4

THE BLIND LEADING THE BLIND

Can the blind lead the blind? A blind man will not allow another blind to lead him except he does not mind falling into the first ditch they come across. It is unusual for the blind to lead the blind. If we are to raise children who are to believe the word, which is preached to them as true, then we must be ready to be good examples of the word. Paul said to the Corinthian Church. "Follow me as I follow the Lord Jesus". Children are like new empty cassette or floppy disk waiting to be filled with messages. They will pick up any message right or wrong from their parents and anyone close enough for them to watch.

The word of God say

Deut 6:20-25
"And when thy son asketh thee in time to come, saying, what mean the testimonies, and the statutes, and the judgements,

31

which the LORD our God has commanded you? Then thou shalt say unto thy son, We were Pharaoh's bondmen in Egypt; and the LORD brought us out of Egypt with a mighty hand: And the Lord shewed signs and wonders great and sore, upon Egypt, upon Pharaoh, and upon all his household, before our eyes: And he brought us out from thence, that he might bring us in, to give us the land which he sware unto our fathers. And the Lord commanded us to do all these statutes, to fear the Lord our God, for our good always, that he might preserve us alive, as it is at this day. And it shall be our righteousness, if we observe to do all these commandments before the Lord our God, as he hath commanded us.

Some years ago as the leader of the Children's Church, I was led one Sunday to visit some children at home. While going through their tape collection I discovered a secular and indecent tape already destroyed. The children confessed that they destroyed their parent's tape because they were not edified with the music, which the parents claimed to have bought for them.

What kind of example are you to your children? If you gossip right in front of them, you do not have any moral justification to ask them to return any itestolen from school. By the way how would you know there is a stolen item when you never find time to check their school bags?

The story of Noah is a perfect example to us. Noah found grace in the sight of God and God asked him to build the ark that would separate his entire family from destruction that was to come on the rest of the world. He was a just man and perfect in his generation. Nothing contrary was mentioned about his sons before the flood, which makes me believe they were just too. God spoke to their father and they were not rebellious to the not-so-reasonable story about the ark. Noah and his wife must have been parents worthy of emulation. When parents have double standards, there is a very high tendency for rebellion to be found in the heart of their children.

New Testament examples of good parents are two

lovely women, Lois and Eunice, the granny and the mother respectively of Timothy the Bishop. Paul said of them:

> 2 Timothy 1:5
> *"When I call to remembrance the unfeigned faith that is in thee (Timothy), which dwelt first in thy grandmother Lois, and thy mother Eunice; and I am persuaded that in thee also."*

Paul in effect was saying theirs was a sincere faith, which they prayerfully passed down the family. Timothy, of course, did not inherit Christianity, he believed the Lord through the word preached to him and the example set by our dear sisters. You may say that it is difficult to live your life daily knowing that, if you look behind your shoulders there are two little eyes watching to see your next action. Don't be discouraged but remember that you can do all things through Christ who strengthens you. Being a good example is part of "all things" that Christ can make you do.

Parents should be rooted in the word of God in order to give sound doctrinal answers to children's questions because children tend to form their opinion based on the answers they get to their questions. For instance, the children in my Sunday school wanted to know if there would be three gods when we get to heaven because of teachings they had heard on the Trinity. Do not forget that they have very wide imagination and expect answers to everything that comes to their mind. Children want answers about sex, dating, sexuality etc and when they do not get answers from home, they take any junk that teachers and friends can give to them.

I was shocked when a minister at one of our prayer conferences catalogued the details of sex lessons curriculum which is already being taught to children between ages five to fifteen in Scotland with the proposal of starting it in England. (We have prayed and trust God that this will not be so) Examples include role-play of the use of condoms and masturbation for children aged seven to eleven. Join me to say God forbid.

We live in dangerous times and the battle for the children and youth in our generation is fiercer than it has ever been. Parents wake up please before it is too late. They do not need to hear about sexuality and other related matters from outsiders especially from friends who may disjoint and spice the truth to suit worldly and individual tastes. May God help us Amen. Ask the Lord for wisdom to take care of His heritage.

CHAPTER 5

PHARAOH'S STRATEGY

Exodus10:8-11

"And Moses and Aaron were brought again unto Pharaoh: and he said unto them, go, serve the Lord your God: but who are they that shall go? And Moses said, we will go with our young and with our old, with our sons and with our daughters, with our flocks and with our herds we will go; for we must hold a feast unto the Lord. And he said unto them, let the Lord be so with you, as I will let you go, and with your little ones: look to it; for evil is before you. Not so: go now ye that are men, and serve the Lord: for that ye did desire. And they were driven out of Pharaoh's presence".

The above story typifies Pharaoh's strategy. This is a concerted effort by the devil to discourage you from taking your children into the Promised Land. Serving

God is supposed to be a family affair. God's stand is that His Spirit will be poured out on all flesh and all flesh includes children. In the above scripture, Moses and Aaron had gone to seek Pharaoh's consent to take all children of Israel out of Egypt to go and worship God but Pharaoh threatened them and offered various subtle and compromising alternatives. Reading the scriptures further, we notice that Pharaoh granted permission to all the men to go and worship but to leave their children and livestock behind. The devil is a liar and the father of all lies and his strategy has not changed and never will. I praise God that as children of God we have wisdom to overcome the wiles and lies of the devil.

Moses refused Pharaoh's strategy and you should too. Today, the devil still gives a million reasons why children should be left at home and not get involved in God's work. These reasons include

- They are noisy and they distract parents at church and it is best to leave them at home to allow us focus in church.
- Having children in the car when there is traffic on the way to church makes them irritable.
- They are young and will not understand.
- They need to grow up first to make up their mind about God.

- They need to stay home, relax, do their homework and sleep on time. While they need to do all these things a good Christian parent needs the wisdom to balance this issue. They do not have to be in church every night of the week either.

Satan would encourage Christians to keep serving God without their children because he knows that with the passage of time we may not be able to bring them back to the Lord. There are many parents today who are going through heartaches, which they would have avoided yesterday. It is not too late to change things. Jesus said:

> Luke 18:16
>
> *"........ Suffer little children to come unto me, and forbid them not: for of such is the kingdom of God"*

The Bible also declares:

> Ecclesiastics 12:1
>
> *"Remember now thy creator in the days of thy youth, while the evil days come not, nor the years draw nigh, when thou shalt say I have no pleasure in them"*

The story of Moses again comes to my mind. Amram and Jochebed, the parents of Moses were among the parents who heard the verdict to kill all Hebrew male children in Egypt. When Jochebed conceived and had a son (Moses), she had an option to offer him to Pharaoh and avoid his wrath. Jochebed could have reasoned at least that she had two other children (Aaron and Miriam) and other parents had given up the right of their children to live to Pharaoh without any struggle. We can make this conclusion because the Bible did not record there was any fight with Pharaoh over this decree.

Today many parents still sacrifice their children at Pharaoh's altar. They give up even before a fight. Have you too given up on your children and teenagers without a fight? My brethren when a child begins to behave in a manner that is outside God's will, it is not the time to give up on that child but rather it is the time for prayer and don't stop praying until something happens. Mothers (and daddies too) when women pray something happens.

Moses' mother saw that her child was a "goodly" child and knew he was not the kind of child for

Pharaoh's sword. What do you see in your child? I once saw a two-month old baby wearing a T-shirt with the inscription "Here comes little devil". The parent saw the devil in their child. How can we blame that child if he grows up to act out what the parents have called him, maybe unintentionally? Such parents have fallen into Pharaoh's subtle strategy. Have you?

Pharaoh's strategy is very subtle and always comes in disguise. Of course if the devil comes with two horns, a tail and a fork people will know him for who he is and shun his counsel but satan is a master with wiles and tricks. He subtly deceives even Christian parents and comes in the guise of books, films, cartoons that promote witchcraft and occultism. This may include materials like Harry Potter books, pokemon, Sabrina the teenage witch etc. Satan has not changed and the spirit of Pharaoh still moves around the earth looking for parents who will directly or indirectly offer the necks of their children to his sword.

Today the devil presents peer pressure, drugs, failure, poverty to mention just a few, right in the face of our children. Will we join hands with our children and overcome the strategies of the enemy or do we fold our hands to watch and see Satan claim God's heritage? What account would you give to the master of our stewardship- Jesus Christ?

Nuggets On How To Conquer Pharaoh's Strategy

- Always remember that your children are God's heritage and you are a caretaker.
- All good and perfect gifts come from God and your children are "goodly" gifts from the Lord.
- Like Amram and Jochebed, determine not to give up your children to Pharaoh and God will always make a way of escape.
- Determine that you and your household will serve the Lord no matter the cost.
- Have listening hearts and ears. Your children need a friendly ally they can share their innermost worries with. They need someone to encourage them after they have been called names at school for not joining the crowd.
- Most importantly, your children need a peaceful home, where love and respect reigns between parents and the fear of God is supreme.

CHAPTER 6

KNOWING YOUR CHILD

I was with a lady once at the hairdressers, when she suddenly jumped out of her seat. She came back a few minutes later with her crying child and she explained she heard the cry of the baby who was in the next house. I thought to myself that this is a mother who really knows her child. Many of us know the sound of our car horns (even our friends' car), the sound of our boss's footsteps, but when our children are stressed out or are going through depression or any issues at all, we are unable to recognise it. Think for a moment - do you really know your child?

> I Kings 3:19-21
> *"And this woman's child died in the night: because she overlaid it. And she arose at midnight, and took my son from beside me, while thine handmaid slept, and laid it in her bosom, and she laid her dead child in my bosom. And when I woke up to give my child suck behold it was dead: but when I considered it in the morning,*

behold, it was not my son, which I did bear".

This is a very key story in the bible that demonstrated God's wisdom through Solomon and exalted him to fame. Solomon's wisdom helped determine who the real mother of the child was. My question however has always been, why did the mother not wake up during the entire night to check the well being of her three days old baby until it was morning. As a parent, are you like this woman? Are you waiting until the devil has gone very far with your children before you arise? God forbid. Make this confession right now, meaning every word that you say " I am not a sleeping Handmaiden. I am a prayerful and watchful parent over my children"

Although the harlot mother was negligent because she slept through the night without attending to her child, she had a positive side to her in that she knew her child even though the child was only three days old. We can conclude that she knew her child from her profound statement '…..but when I considered it in the morning, behold it was not my son which I did bear'. She 'considered' her child and she could not be fooled by the other harlot. You may know your child's best dress or meal but do you really know your child in the things that matter most? Are you in a position to stand in defence of your child and say "I know my child, he or she cannot do this."?

You must know your children, their likes, dislikes, and be ready to guide them by the word of God into the way of truth. Learn to notice changes in your children even when these changes may look insignificant, for example sudden unusual closeness to another child or adult or a sudden change in the way a child walks. Did you know that statistics has it that child molesters are usually not strangers but people that the victim has known and is comfortable with. When two children suddenly get unusually close, try to find out what the common interest is. The motive or secret behind their relationship should direct you on whether to encourage the friendship or not. A few times of course, you may just be crying wolf where really there is no wolf amongst the sheep.

If a shy child suddenly begins to "bounce" around, it may be worth knowing why. Ask the Holy Spirit to help you to identify the new excitement. As a

Christian parent you must not be too busy to listen to our kids, their fears, worries and aspirations. Professional child carers are taught to carefully observe children in their care for only ten minutes every week and to write down the activities of the children during that time. I tried doing this with a child in my care once and it is amazing the kind of things you notice when you really take time to look.

Knowing your children will definitely help you to know their capabilities and ensure they are not forced to do things outside their areas of interest but rather to prayerfully guide them into the plan and purpose of God for their lives. The harlot mother we read about learnt a good lesson from this experience. Thank God she turned around quickly as you will notice, she wanted her child to live under any circumstance although the other harlot wanted the child dead. Your children shall not die but they shall live to declare the works of God in the land of the living. Amen.

CHAPTER 7

WHAT ABOUT DISCIPLINE?

Note that discipline is the word and not punishment. Discipline is derived from the word 'disciple' – which means systematic training in obedience to cause improved behaviour. Discipline is very challenging as opportunities for discipline will present themselves to a parent on a daily if not hourly basis, in the little areas like sit here, tidy your room, who sits where and who plays with what toys.

You cannot overlook the things that your children do, under the guise of love. You cannot love them more than God loves them.

> Hebrew 12:5 – 8
> *"And ye have forgotten the exhortation which speaketh unto you as unto children. My son, despise not thou the chastening of the Lord, nor faint when thou art rebuked of him: For whom the Lord loveth, he Chasteneth, and scourgeth every son whom he receiveth. If ye endure*

chastening, God deals with you as with sons; for what son is he whom the father chasteneth not, whereof all are partakers, then are ye bastards, and not sons".

A child that is not disciplined most likely will not turn out right. We look on the streets of our cities and see bunches of children who have not been trained and never disciplined.

The discipline of your child should be an expression of love aimed at improving their behaviour and must not be seen as vengeance for whatever they have done. Discipline should not be punitive but should be used as a deterrent from bad behaviour. Families are encouraged to adopt a procedure where they first of all create an awareness of acceptable and clear right and wrong attitude so everyone knows the rule of the game from day one. Of course, these rules should have been made by all the family before implementation.

The kids will find it easier if they have been part of the process of making the 'laws'. Without you pointing out the discipline required the children themselves would remind each other of the consequences of any wrong action. That way disciplinary action can be seen as fair. Let there be a clear definition of what is wrong and what is right and the source of standards which is the Holy Bible should not be confused either. Let the entire family be aware it is God's standards.

Try prayer as prayer changes things. Discipline is spiritual parental duty and should be handled as such. That means you cannot discipline your children in the flesh otherwise it becomes punitive and not corrective or deterrent. The Holy Spirit has a way of ministering to us when we have been naughty. He can speak so clearly to your child that the conviction of what they have done will be so strong on them without you doing or saying anything at all. You can win the battle first on your knees and not by shouting and howling at the kids. That can only result in cracked voices and offensive exchanges with your children. We do not wrestle against flesh and blood and the weapon of our warfare are not carnal but mighty through God to the pulling down of strongholds. (Ephesians 6:12).

What kind of child is your child? Children born of the same parents and raised under the same environment and with the same resources available would sometimes turnout different. Some are strong willed, disruptive and others just passive and would do whatever mama and papa say. For whatever kind of child the Lord has blessed you with, be sure you need wisdom to discipline both. Like James Dobson says in His book **Solid Answers** "Don't let them get too far from you emotionally. Stay in touch. Don't write them off, even when your impulse is to do just that. They need you more than ever before"

We must endeavour to be firm in correcting our children. They are smart and know when either parent is weak and would fall for their whims. The laws in a family make more sense when both parents believe the course and are ready to back it. Your children should believe that they would get the same response on every issue from either parent.

Favouritism should be avoided like a plague. God will give you the ability and wisdom to love them equally, never letting any child feel out of place at home. Of course, issue of age, nature and ability for the different kids would always come to play but much care should be taken to avoid "glaring" favouritism. A good example is where the young child who is crying is allowed to play with the toy of an older child. For this you may need to carefully explain the reason why one has been preferred to the other.

Before any disciplinary action is taken ask questions to know why the child has done that which he is about to be disciplined for. Classify what the child has done wrong. Is it negotiable or not? Life threatening or not. If a child keeps trying to do things that are not scriptural you know that is non-negotiable and the child should be disciplined. E.g. lying and trying to cover up for it. Are they always trying to fall into the hands of every stranger that comes their way? That could be life threatening. When you discipline, are you revenging or are you doing it with a mind to change them? What standard is the yardstick for discipline, yours or God's? Was the offence intentional? In the mind of the child was he trying to do good? Lack of knowledge? The response to this will determine the gravity of correction applied. If you think they are deliberately trying to annoy you, then you may react forcefully.

It is important to match the offence with the correction. The correction applied should not out-weigh the offence. Otherwise, the child may misconstrue your good gesture as evil. Imagine a child who has just eaten a good meal and begin to jump around restlessly. If we only realise that he only seeks a way to burn off excess energy, then our chastising will be tempered with mercy instead of with bitterness.

Now the question you have been waiting for. **How should I discipline?** My first reaction is; What does the bible say? We have to first of all agree that the bible is our standard.

Proverbs 22:6
"Train up a child in the way he should go: and when he is old he will not depart from the Lord".

Proverbs 29:15
"The rod and reproof give wisdom, but a child left to himself bringeth shame to his mother".

Proverbs 13:24
"He that spareth the rod hateth his son: but he that loveth him chasteneth him betimes".

Proverbs 22:15
"Foolishness is bound in the heart of a

child; but the rod of correction will remove it far from him"

Proverbs 23:13-14
"Withhold not correction from the child: for if thou beatest him with the rod, he shall not die. Thou shalt beat him with the rod and he shall deliver his soul for hell".

Proverbs 29:17
"Correct thy son, and he shall give thee rest: yea he shall give delight unto thy soul".

Ephesians 6: 1-3
"Children obey your parents in the Lord for this is right. Honour your father and mother which is the first commandment with a promise that it may be well with you and that you may live long on the earth"

From the above scriptures, am I suggesting that you spank your children with every opportunity that comes your way? NO. I do not think too that the bible suggests that you spank them for every reason possible. As a parent you cannot misuse your authority over your children. We cannot rule out spanking either. It is important to first of all pray and bind whatever spirits that continue to influence your children, and guiding them by the word of God because the word gives understanding to the simple. Spanking should be okay but this should be as infrequent as can be and really for very serious offences that are non-negotiable and maybe life threatening but please do no spank for every little offence. Not only will it make your correction common and nonsensical but also you could as a parent become abusive. The issue of to spank or not to spank is a very fine line which you should with the help of the Holy Spirit learn to draw.

One Sunday morning, during my teaching at my Sunday school class, I felt the need to tell the children I loved them. A couple of them smiled and welcomed my love story but a handful did not budge. They were not impressed at all with my love talk. Then I said, " it looks like some of you do not believe me". We had always agreed to be frank with each other and so they answered in the affirmative. They said if I loved them, I would not spank them or correct them the way I did sometimes. We had to search the scripttur and after reading about twenty scriptures on correction and the rod, one of them jokingly said, "Sister Marj, you really love us, you have never tried the rod".

Other Suggested Disciplinary Measures Could Be:

. Stopping them from going to a social outing they would really have loved to attend.
. Scolding by word of mouth and counselling (not sharp reproof except where deemed necessary)
. Withholding a very longed for gift (for a while)
. Please do not withhold meals, as a corrective measure will not change the attitude of your child It will either aggravate rebellion and hatred against parents

I grew up under very strict discipline and my parents spanked us, sometimes with the'rod'. I saw both sides of discipline: correction and punishment. While my mother will sue the'rod', then a good explanation for why you had to be spanked would usually follow and then a little reconciliatoryy gift, my dad was different. He was of few words but mant good strokes. Today, I look on to those times without the old intensive bitternes because I know mow that was his own way of making sure all his children, especially the girls turned out right and not bring him shame. He had carved out a name as a strict disciplinarian at the institution where he was the head and wanted to make sure his own kids turned out right. I never enjoyed the strokes from my dad and I still believe he could have passed across his message without those strokes.

CHAPTER 8

FINALLY...

Know Your Parental Responsibilities

God has given the duty of parenting and child upbringing to the parents. As a parent you are supposed to love, care and bring your children to maturity in the things of God. Sunday school teachers, Pastors, Nannies and Au pairs etc are only helps in this great task. God said this of Abraham:

> Genesis 18:19
> *"For I know him, that he will command his children and his household after him, and they shall keep the way of the Lord, to do justice and Judgement; that the Lord will bring upon Abraham that which he hath spoken of him."*

God wants to speak the same about you. Abraham

commanded his children and household to follow the Lord God even after his death. So also you can leave behind a "bunch of Christians" (Christ-like people) as we are often referred to. Leave no doubt in the hearts of your children that there is no other way except the way of the Lord. Your family needs to know that there is no other option but to serve the Lord our God. Even when they stray from the path of life our prayer for salvation and Restoration must continue until we see God glorified in their lives. Like Joshua we shall be saved and our household too.

Teach Your Children

We are to teach our children "diligently", taking responsibility for raising them as good citizens and a people being made ready for heaven. Let any time you spend with your children be 'quality time'. Ensure your children learn something about God every time you are with them. Every opportunity that presents itself should be utilised as a step towards their godly upbringing.

The Bible says we should *"train up a child in the way he should go and when he is old, he will not depart from it"*. (Pro 22:6)

Deuteronomy 6:5-9

" And thou shalt love the Lord thy God with all thy heart............thou shalt teach them diligently unto thy children, and shall talk of them when thou sittest in thine house, and when thou walkest by the way, and when thou liest down, and when thou risest. And thou shalt bind them for a sign upon thine hand, they shall be as frontlets between thine eyes. And thou shall write them upon the post of thy house, and on thy gates"

Our family lives should be centred on the Lord Jesus. When we sit at home, our time should be used to glorify the Lord rather than discuss and run down our friends, pastors, school teachers, etc. Discuss the law of the Lord otherwise your children will copy these negative things and make you ashamed in future. Thoughts are governed by what we hear, watch, read and the association we keep, for as a man thinks in his heart so is he. You must watch what you do around your children and avoid corrupt communications from your lips because children are very fast at taking in what they see people who are in authority over them do.

Do Not Provoke Your Children

Ephesians 6:4

"And fathers do not provoke your children to wrath: but bring them up in the nurture and admonition of the Lord"

I presume that many will be surprised that God says the children should not be provoked to anger because we have quietly almost believed that children have no emotions and really have no mind of their own. Remember they are humans too. In what ways do you provoke your children to anger? Consistently telling a child how worthless he or she is would provoke him or her. When only a child's mistakes and faults are put before him or her with no encouragement coming from the parents, he or she can be provoked to anger. The most likely result of provocation is rebellion. Even when a child errs, that child should be corrected in love.

Discipline Your Children

Proverbs 13:24

"He that spareth his rod hateth his

son: but he that loveth him chasteneth him betimes"

A lot has been said about discipline in chapter seven but I will like to emphasise that discipline is not just a set of rules and regulations for your children rather, it is systematic training in the walk of obedience. In addition, when you correct a child do not forget to say why. Tell them what the issue is but please do not yell at them.

Provide For Your Children

Matthew 7:9-10
"Or what man is there of you, whom if his son ask bread, will he give him a stone? Or if he ask a fish, will he give him a serpent?"

As caretakers we have a duty to provide the good things of life for our children. A good education in today's world is a must and parents have to ask God in his infinite mercies to provide for the upkeep of their children. As parents we are not to wear the best clothes, ride posh cars at the expense of our children's education, health and feeding. Children do not have to practically crawl on their knees to get any thing from their parents but this is no license to unwisely lavish them with things either. Having children was a choice that you made at one time or the other, so you cannot start considering the cost (real or opportunity cost) of taking care of them now.

Plan For Your Children's Future

> Proverbs 13:22
> *"A good man leaveth an inheritance to his children's children: and the wealth of the sinner is laid up for the just"*

Plan to leave a good inheritance for your children. You cannot do this if you pile up debts for them. The son of the prophet who piled up debts for his family in 2 Kings 4:1-6 almost mortgaged the lives of his children but for the divine intervention of God. Piling up debts today is a way of mortgaging the lives and future of your children as against leaving them an inheritance. There are so many types of investments available today, call your bank, building society or investment adviser to make enquiries. While some of the things we spend our money on depreciate in value very fast (like cars, clothes, toys etc) some others appreciate in value (like houses, shares in blue chip companies, etc.) In the United Kingdom all parents receive child benefits for each child. While some parents spend this for toys and clothes, others invest this same amount towards the future of their children. If you save this sum of about £60.00 weekly for over a period of sixteen years at an interest of say 2% per annum, your child would receive £13,586. This makes_good sense to me. There are lots of Christian materials available that will surely bless you with the wisdom on how to leave an inheritance for your children and children's children. Look for them and also seek financial advice from your bankers.

Be Your Children's Friend

In some homes the parents are so unreachable that their children scurry in fright once they hear their parents voices or the hoot of their car. Learn to show a smiling face around the house because the children remember the smiling face wherever they go and would do everything in their power not to hurt that face with any "bad news". This is my testimony. Many times I avoided negative peer pressure because I always remembered the smiling face of my mother and I never wanted any "bad news" to come home to her, knowing that it would break her heart.

Be A Good Example To Your Children

Children learn by the example you set as an authority over them. Be careful to be a good example. Kneel by their bedside daily and pray with them. They will never find prayer and study of the word burdensome if they start early. Let your conversation be pure.

Arguments between spouse should not be before the children. It is amazing how some spouses quarrel before their children and reconcile behind closed doors. You may have made up with your spouse behind but in the hearts of your children the quarrel still persists except you reconcile in their presence.

Nuggets On Child Upbringing

- Pray and study the word daily with your children
- Teach them to memorise scriptures and verses
- Treat every child specially for they are special to God.
- Teach them to select good friends, television programmes, books etc ......Be interested in what they watch.
- Testify always of the goodness of the Lord in your home.
- Christian character building books should be provided for your children even though they may end being torn up and destroyed. (forgive those that tear these books for they know not what they do. They will learn when it is their turn to pay. You learnt too).

Conclusion

I have enjoyed writing this little book and not just that, I have been blessed too! However, before I conclude I would like to leave a word with two classes of people who may read this book.

Firstly, those that have children and have put in all efforts to make these children what God wants them to be and it seems nothing at all is working. God's word says in Ephesians 6:13b-14 "...having done all, to stand. Stand therefore,..." God's will is that we do not give up. I encourage you to hold on until you see breakthrough. Keep loving them even if they continue breaking your heart. Both parents should decide that for them it is BATTLE that will be conquered on their knees.

For those waiting on the Lord for their children, God remains ever faithful. His word is Yea and Amen. Don't be weary, keep holding on. What He has done for one, He will do for you also.

A good decision to make is not to stay hurt or wounded when you realise that almost everyone except you and your spouse has an explanation for why you still do not have a child. Some may say it is because you have no faith and other may say it is because you have unforgiveness in your heart, while another category may say maybe like Michal who despised David her husband you have despised your husband. Some go as far as saying it could be your punishment for your sin of abortion. Look around you and not too far from you are unbelievers who do not know God and who do all the listed things above and God still blessed them with children. Girlfriend, the point I am making is bad things sometimes happens to good people and sometimes good things also happen to 'bad people'

Get busy in the house of the Lord and do not quit from your labour of love. God rewards diligence and children are the reward from the Lord. He will surely reward in due season if you faint not. Remember everyday that there is no barren in the house of God for "He maketh the barren woman to keep house, and to be a joyful mother of children "**(Psalm 113:9)**. God is not a partial God for what He makes happen for one person He will do for others also, since He is without any injustice.

God bless you!

About the Author

Pastor Marjorie Esomowei can best be described as a woman who loves the Lord. She is a gifted teacher of the word, a motivator and an intercessor. She feels a deep sense of call to women and children and strives to be an encouragement to them. Her greatest passion is to bring out the best in other people. Pastor Marjorie is co-pastor of Triumphant Church International and the president of Triumphant Women Ministries, a ministry arm of women in Triumphant Church International. She is the host of the annual Triumphant Women's Conference, the Strategic Women's School of Wisdom and the "When Women Pray" Prayer Conference. She has held crusades and conferences in Gabon, Ghana, Uganda, Nigeria, Scotland, United Kingdom, blessing many by the wisdom of the word of God.

She has a BSc (Hons) Degree in Economics and is an Alumnus of Institute of Management Development, Lausanne. She is married to Reverend Clement Esomowei, who is Pastor of Triumphant Church International (Destiny Ministries). Pastor Marjorie joined her husband in full time ministry leaving behind a very successful banking career with one of Nigeria's foremost investment banks. She has authored "Overcoming in Gilgal" Her husband and herself now reside in England

Prayer Confession

STARTING A GENERATION
THAT IS BLESSED

I am a virtuous woman. Today I set in motion a prophetic word that goes into my future. I declare that I start a generation of blessing like Joseph. I wear the commanded "blessing" on me and it is going down to everyone in my generation after me.

Psalm 112 - God Says my seed shall be mighty on the face of the earth and my seed shall be blessed. I claim this blessing for my myself, my husband, all our children and for our children's children. Wealth and riches shall always be in my house, in my present family and down to my generations to come.

Light shall appear to us wherever there was darkness. Every darkness in our lives disappears today, for darkness cannot comprehend/withstand the light of God in us.

According to **Psalm 12:5** – I am a good woman and I order all my affairs with discretion and prudence. I am a wise builder and from today my family is blessed with wisdom. The spirit of wisdom is going down my bloodline. It is going down my bloodline for generations to come.

According to **Psalm 145:4 -** the praise of God Almighty shall continue from one generation to another. The fear of God runs through my family line from one generation to another. No member of my bloodline will live outside the fear of the Lord. I shall serve the Lord with my entire household.

Psalm 14:5 – says God is in the generation of the righteous. I declare that so shall it be in my family. God will be in all that we do. God is in my home, my marriage and all that concerns me.

Genesis 24:60 – And they blessed Rebecca and said "Our sister, may you become the mother of thousands and ten thousands and may your descendants possess the gates of those who hate them". This is my portion from today. My descendant will no longer be defeated; they will possess the gates of those who hate them.

Ruth 4:11 – Says I shall be like Leah and Rachel who built the house of Israel and made the tribe of Ephraim famous. From today I declare that I am a builder and I will make the name of my father and husband famous, wherever I go.

Psalm 37:25 - Like David, I have not seen the righteous forsaken nor his seed beg for bread. My seed shall not be forsaken, they shall not beg for bread, both now in the future and forever. As in Psalm 37: 19, in the time of famine, we shall all be satisfied. We shall not lack in Jesus mighty name I pray.

Proverbs 11:21 – Says the posterity of the righteous shall be delivered. My seed and I shall be delivered in every situation that comes against us. We are delivered from plague, from calamity, from false doctrines, drug addiction, alcoholism, and terrorism in the mighty name of Jesus I Pray. Amen.